AF259033

Acknowledgement of Country

I acknowledge the Traditional Custodians of the land on which this work was written and created, the Turrbal and Yugara peoples of Meanjin, and I pay my deep respects to their Elders, past, present, and emerging.

I honour their unbroken connection to land, language, story, and culture, and recognise that sovereignty was never ceded.

I extend this respect to all First Nations peoples across Australia, whose voices, histories, and creative traditions continue to guide and enrich this place.

Curses of Verses:

A Composite

by

By M Renae Dubois

Introduction

The following is the poetic, in-the-moment accounting of my journey, after a brain injury at 16 years old, from young woman to poet, artist and eventual philosopher. This work is the cumulation of three biographical verse-novels that I wrote over 35 years. They examine the search for identity I undertook, and the tests I confronted daily. My ethical metal had always been at odds with my surrounding religious, medical, legal, and social dynamics, and my newfound personality did, and does not allow for unexamined ambiguities.

With and without my more recent, polished poetic technique, I write about my work in the sex industry candidly, unapologetically, and at times with humour. I have traditionally considered myself to be without clear bias, but recently I have had to take into account my probable privileged experience, of working by choice, independently, and legally. This time lasted sporadically for over 30 years. My experience with this line of work, despite my privilege is no less compelling or worthy of philosophical, sociological, or psychological consideration.

This work started as an attempt to explain myself, to my lawyers, the health community, my friends, relationships, my parents. By the 3rd in this series, I am no longer seeking this, and instead am presenting myself, my impressions, and my perspectives. This book, a composite of my first 3 books, ends with some pure story telling fiction.

2026 M Renae Dubois

Contents

Head Injury:

Pros and Cons

Ode to Koffies

The clatter of the combination
Of cafe crowd and coffee espresso
Kept a continuous cacophony
Of controlled chaos.

The populace of particulars
Postured pretentiously,
Playing at the picture of
Post-pubescent parody.

Simmering, my spirit
Stung in the symphony as
Suspicion and scorn
Swelled in my soul.

Beginning

I had a major head injury,

A coma for a week

I was driving with a family friend

Hit a truck on narrow street

Now I've left my high school

I've got a job as well

But I can't control my wayward mouth

And my burning inner swell

Claret

As I sit with glass in front of me,
I am inclined to think
Of all that lies ahead of me
Including this foul drink

I'd like to be an artist
But I am no good at art
I'd like to be a composer
Cause music's in my heart

Talentless, I feel I am
I don't know where to go
Working retail, selling shoes
Looking people in the toe

Do I want to drink this stuff?
Is wine my vice to be?
An artist suffers everyday
Can see that will be me

But what's my music I don't know

What's my favourite kind of art?

Oh hell, too hard, I think I'll go and

Have a drink and be a tart

Beginnings

I suppose you want to know about me
Who I really am,
I'll tell you more as you go on
Of where I all began

Now to suffice – I'm seventeen
A virgin only just
Left school after knock on head
Giving everyone my trust

There is a magic innocence
It has a witch-like stare
It's complex and confusing
Not appealing so to bare

For now, read on, you'll discover more
Of where I found to go
I'll give you hints – there's a word in there
That rhymes with lo, roe, joe, woah, foe

Slutsky

The guy I did the other day
Found me stumbling up the mall
He left the girl he'd cornered there
A chat-up he would take the fall

To take me to a nightclub
Buy me another drink
I didn't even want one
But didn't choose to think

Since then I've done a bouncer
A streetie, and a yob
I'm losing touch with feeling
But it's easy to please a nob

Mrs Fields Cookies

"Hereya, have three"

"Of these Brownies, you're sure?"

"Yeah take them you're hungry

Do you want some more?"

"No, wow so good of you,

What time do you close?"

"We close when the centre shuts

Then I hit the road"

"To home you mean?"

"Well yeah for a while

But only so I can change

And go out in style"

"Where do you go?"

"To raves and the Beat.

They once had a slippery dip

And spa for your feet!"

"I'll have to go check this out

What is your name?"

"You can call me on this number

And Jason's my name."

Fortitude Valley

The valley is full of
Crusties and nerds
They all are escaping
From the city herd

But to escape in the valley?
Still, it's a thrill
And I'm here, so there you go
I know the will

The source of enjoyment
In being yourself
The valley forces you
To work it, to hell

With the rest
What do they know?
We all are in limbo
And in the flow

Strut it, Work it
Show us your stuff
If you think you're so good
Then smooth over the rough

Do you have something
That exceeds the rest?
I believe you, no really!
But I'm still the best

At least in my own mind
And that's where it lies
The panic of initiation
Mutates into thrive

And once you have got it
Don't ever give in
Cause you can take it
Wherever you sin.

Ladies

Pretty features
Muted clothes
The talk is chirping
Not overblown

The excitement accentuated
By gurgling slurs
The voices intermingle
The words unheard

A quiet descends
And tension is sensed
The girls don't like anyone
Who's too intense

Mistress of madness
Sitting alone
The latte growing colder
The cigarette blown

Fairy lights

Jingle stills

Coffee crowd

And crystal bells

Ladies make the

Night light flow

In happy enchantment

The magic shows.

The magic is broken

A guest has spoken

"Hey Hey its Saturday"

Destroys any token

Of sophisticated company

And class in style

The media impact

Has not raised a smile

Luckily the waitress

Intervenes on time

And those who know better

Find a new rhyme.

Journal #11

It makes sense to make a go of
Prostitution for a change
I'm fucking all these idiots
I may as well make some real gains

Golden Girls or VIP
Doesn't matter – all the same
I did a night - it worked out well
I get there on the train

Five days down, still no regrets
Expecting it to get better yet
I'll work from Sydney, yeah, I know!
I'll find a parlour and a flat to let

No one should know that I'm leaving
No one would like me to go
I'll have to take that dingy car
Get to Sydney, be a ho.

"I'm working"

"I started, Jay
I started the job
Seven hundred dollars down
It's no fucking slog

Yes, I do females too
No I don't spank
Well not as a permanent thing
Just as a wank

Jay stop all this bullshit
When you gonna start
You told me we'd do it
Put it into my heart

Whatever you are gonna do
I'm having a good time
It doesn't seem disgusting
Nor like a warning sign

Sydney Bound

I stole that car – my boyfriend's car
The one I got my license on
A Torana, red is what I've got
To get to Sydney, on the run

It's Byron Bay, there's people here
Who want to come with me down south
They can drive my car, and share the load
And who knows, they might even shout

Arduous this journey is
And in this car it's not real safe
Coffs Harbour now; I wonder how
Long it's gonna take

Aah, we made it here, I see the bridge
Let's cross it now, and seal our night
If we just choose the right lane - oh shit
What was the fucking point?

A bloody tunnel - great

What a style to start the stay

Misdirection; under the bridge

Why is this always my way?

Stay positive; stay upbeat now

It won't do to get depressed

This is a big progression and

You can't afford to fail the test

Glamour

Terrace house
Decked to the hilt
There's no hint of trash
In the curtains of silk

This is what I knew
Sydney was for
A sex workers paradise
Open for all

I'm loving the sex
Loved to be slut!
But there's no money in fucking around
Free sex is a stupid rut

I like their machismo
Although most men are foul
But their easier than women
Who are smart and cruel

So I've become a hermit

If you can call it that

I stay in my beautiful parlour

And fuck them till they're flat

I fuck them hard; I make them work

At the moment I'm on my back

But when they're gone I get a thrill

And add money to the stack

Of things that God has given me

Just for being alive

In this sordid industry

My twisted ego thrives.

Sydney is down

"There you go, you fucking slut
Rub that on your gums
Cocaine will see what you have got"
Or if it's you that I will shun.

"Not that way, bitch - stupid slut,
Why don't you get a life?
I'm paying for your drugs right here
You're gonna get me into strife."

"I didn't actually want this
I wasn't in the mood
You got me at a real bad time
I wasn't ready, dude"

"We're going for a walk right now,
Why don't you come along"
Stumbling, I followed after them
In a daze I brought the bong

I shudder now to think of it

How messy that all was,

Some fucking bitch got me with that shit

She was too high to give a toss

Right in my lounge room,

Right after work,

I'd had a bad day as it was

I didn't need this jerk

Sydney

Platforms and fishnets
Mascara and mini
My hair was dishevelled
My eyes were spinning

In 10.30 glare
On Wednesday morning
All I wanted was coffee
To stop me yawning

No kettle at home
The thought pissed me off
I walked into Chandlers
And gave a loud cough

"Show me your kettles"
"I want the best"
Brashly and rudely
Fuck the rest.

Coming back

They tell me I should go back
I'm not convinced they're wrong
I'm toying with some scary thoughts
But I haven't been here long

The parlour where I'm working
Is new and really slow
I don't like staying every day
And not bringing in the dough

I need to change my image
I need to move my stuff
I want to be free in a space
Without acting really tough

I want to lose a bit more weight
I want to tone it up
I want to park my car at work
Without getting a ticket stub

I've got these pills - they're Mersyndols

I got two packets to decide

Will I take them all at once

And exit with the tide?

Wuss

"A Bipolar, a Borderline"
"You'll be treated for them now on in.
Medication is what you'll get
And hospital when you're misbehaving"

I feel I should explain myself
Who I am and what I know
This is why I am myself
This is what I feel I know

They tell me my good sense is gone
And that my brain doesn't function right
They've shoved me in a corner
And I don't want to fight

So I'll take my choice of drugs thank you
And I hope I don't get caught
Trial procedures bad enough
The psychiatrists have already wrought...

No, they'll send me to hospital

And tear apart my brain

Peeling off the layers until

They find a conducive vein

Brisbane Again

They got me back -it's not so bad
I'm living with a friend
I've got some sexy pieces
Oblivious to trend

The hairstyle's long and then it's short
The colour changes too
I'm spending all my money
Just to get a new hairdo

I don't know where to start to work
I can't here at my friends
I think I'll go into the mall
See if I can meet some men

I'm thinking hard but errantly
About what I can do next
I'm looking for a dealer though
And I sent someone a text

43

Des

I found a lovely man today
That I've been looking for, for years
I used to know him averagely
But his absence caused no tears

The most professional man I've met
He definitely knows the score
Aware of his face, knows his place
And doesn't ask for more

We're acting on our instincts
And going with the flow
The flow is good
And we both know.

Me

He mentioned sex quite easily

My God we have done well

But I'm a worker so I can't

Just relieve his primal swell

I know he doesn't let himself

Go through with sex at all

But he knew that I wanted it

So he must trust me or he'd stall

I told him that I couldn't sleep

With anyone for free

I told him how that went against

My entire morality

It was the truth - a vow I'd made

Before he came back on my scene

So many people just don't accept

What sex can really mean

Now I feel I'm getting more
Of everything that I want most
This guy's for real, when he sleeps with me
He always puts me first.

Lighting

His passion for history
Moves me deeply
Antiques in his home
Restore the past eerily

A railway clock keeps that time
And these items there
A picture of Queen Vic
And her dogged stare

Couch is leather,
Lamps abound
Every evening at six
Lighting changes round

No more a balcony
With back yard views
Rather tall curtains,
And golden hues

This life is a dream,
The aroma the best
I love my new life
With Des and the rest

Whole Truth

Our relationship is better
Than how it started out
Both of us are talking now
Love and what that's about

That's what we talk about
When we're in bed
Most of the time we're
In each others head

He is in my vision
Every minute of the day
And I know he is watching me
In the same way

Assessing each others images
And how we relate to some
We've gotten a little egotistic
But that is part of the fun

We know we're good people

He says we're the best

We couldn't be though

If you know the rest

June

How do I love
This man of my dreams
He's everything I wanted
It's mutual it seems

But that is a crazy
Illusion of mine
I couldn't be really
The sign of his times

I'm just a girlfriend
And he is my lover
He does what he does
I don't play big brother

To love him I let him
Decide for himself
Although the return of that favour
Is not mutually felt

I don't understand
What he's trying to do
"You said that you wanted
A woman to fit into you!"

Accident Tales

Fuck fuck fuck fuck fuck fuck fuck
I feel like such a jerk
I'm with a loved one in my life
But I still feel I'm in search

In search for stable peace of mind
And what that myth might mean
I think it means that I can handle
Any sort of scene

Head injury at seventeen
A compo battle now
I can't get away from all
The medico-legal rows

The lawyers have taken away my right
To fuck up on my own
The years from which I've learnt the most
Have been spoiled from early on.

Their words, reports and worse
The thought, I cannot write a will
Have driven home their cruelty
In present, past and future still.

Weakday

This morning my feelings
Were confused

My head was dizzy
And my body felt tired

I could not sleep
I did not know what

I wanted to do

So I had a cup of tea
and slept

Within the blanket of
open eyes

My dressing gown did
fall apart

And in a wave my head
fell back

Clunk

Against the wall.

Slowly the eventualness
Pattered at my consciousness
Grinding at my layers
Carving out my soul

Perspective regained in my mind
Gently though at least
A point of view is special
It's all my territory

Only my eyes count for much
It is my brain after all
The truth does slip into place
And now it's my call.

Angrily

I gave up the sex work
Threw myself into you
Not asking for anything
Except something to do

We see my writing
Get better in style
So I cling on to what
Will cause inspiration to rile

But like any artist
(Bored housewife too)
I've been taking narcotics
Not unlike you

I've got my aggression
I can feel the strength grow
Confidence and assertiveness
But I actually know

That I have a habit
Amphetamine time
I'm not feeling bad about it
I'm enjoying my rhyme.

Jason

I've got to get a grip on it
You've got to understand
This is a whole new life for me
I don't want to hold your hand

Jay you think I am a pro
That that is who I am
You've lost the plot and gone all weird
You're strange in your demands

I'm giving up on you my friend
You are not what I need
I need to be a woman now
I don't want to fit your creed

Astronaut

My thoughts are skimming past the surface

Of a romantic dream

In the midst of the confusion

My body followed steam

I am forced to take a step back

And to open up my eyes

In my brain there is a mission

That's what he sees inside

A girl of ambition

Who cannot sit still

It is a fusion

Of body and will

But the trust of my partner

Has become paramount

Have I been looking for someone

To believe in my stunt?

I know I can do it

I believe in my strength

And God, what a struggle

For mental health

I told him about myself

Needing some space

I told him about writing

And getting out of his face

But, no more justifications

A fact is a fact

I shall be leaving this house soon

And getting a flat.

Current Form

Holding back on friendliness

Bringing in the sign

I feel so unattractive though

If I don't pay them for their time

I find though when I pull back

And stay in my own zone

That things can work out perfectly

And in a pleasant tone

I'm a bad girl

And playing at being weak

And alone is not necessary

My boyfriend knows

I am not "spreading my oats"

as he said.

"I already have a crop"

That's what I said

Decisions and Delusions

We did the deed together
We did it really well
We found the perfect home for me
It's mine and we can tell

Art deco style
With plastered ceilings
The rooms are furnished
There's a labyrinthic feeling

It's my little mansion
All I need is, well, everything
But Deszy helped me pay for it
So I'll get the rest through my thing

I don't know how yet
But I feel like a scammer
Maybe I've always been
At least I'm not on the hammer

Raid

I awoke on Saturday afternoon
Naked on Des' bed
He was wandering in and out of there
Clearly using his head

I noticed lots of bags around
The type for Des' bits
His mate, who lived with him as well
Was busy doing sticks

Des came back into the room
And gave me some good news
There was some smack and speed on its way
All for him and me to use

At the door there was a knock
Which Davo went to answer
The cops are here, he ran back to say
And grabbed two bags of hydro

I pulled the sheets to thinly disguise

That I was a naked female

My hair was a mess and I must confess

I chose to play the detail

I must be naive, because an hour ago

I thought they'd let him come home

But I figure that now he's in the watchhouse in town

And they won't let him go near the phone

Confront

He's gone away
Just like that
I cannot hide today

Or any day, I have to do
What's right by him and me
I've got to put a brave face on
Until to the woods I flee

I love him, yes truly
But what are we facing?
Six months, six years
Is the law faking?

He is getting punished
I'm not to share
If I am miserable
He will not care

No I have to be stronger

Than I've ever been

And I'm already failing

And being seen.

Promises

Promised I was worth it
Told that I deserved it
Compensation was put to me
As a reason for how I be

Pain, yeah I'm hurting
Miserable suicidal madness
Is it because of
My head injury?

Sold my soul
Is reality
I sold my belief in myself
For compo money

They've given me false hope in legality
They're not on my side
Psychiatry?

So I'm lonely

I missed your call for fifty bucks

This proves to me that my life sucks

Damaged In Pain

They are low down dirty cunts
I told you so before
This age is now self-seeking, so
There is room for my raw sore

I will let speed enliven my soul
And it's true that it is hard
To remember who you really are
With a needle up your arm

Wacol

The sun on my legs is
Burning warm
The glare from the page
The eye of the storm

There's the mentals, indigenous
The elderly, the kids
The bush bandits, the crusties
And the old man who spits

There's a post box and a Cornetto sign
An overpass and a fence
The railway passes through here
The station is intense

Two general convenience stores
That cater for everyone
The food is semi-edible
But sitting here is fun

I have to wait for twelve you see
To get into the local jail
You know that this is Wacol
And my boyfriend didn't get bail

I have to let them play their game
And we have to follow the system
For what he did they have to push
His head into the cistern

They've got a job to do
And regulations to abide
Des is cut off from the real world
And doesn't feel the tide

He shouldn't feel the tide as such
That's what he's in there for
An extradition from the external world
Life in there must be a bore

Deszy

I don't know what we said today yet

Because I'm waiting to go in

As you know I came this morning

But they wouldn't let me in

I was a little late my love

I hope you weren't distressed

Everything I try to do these days

Turns out a miserable mess

I'm working all the details out

And sorting out your stuff

But people out here think I'm mad

So it is really tough

Not to load all that on you

The worst part about being mad

Is that straight people magnify the detail

And treat me really bad

Still, it's good for me, that attitude

It's time I toughened up

Having you in there and me out here

Had better lead to moving up

Oh No!

The concept of living
To protect my arse
Doesn't seem so bad now
If that's the ask

I'm pretty self-seeking
That's the clue
The realisation is unshocking
They are too

Yeah I'll join your fight
For my right
To be myself
My mouth shut tight

But I can't do that
I know it
So I'll talk in different melody
Same old shit

No emotion, no bare souls

No room for broken hearts

Honesty in untruthfulness

Will take me further fast

Mum and Me

I'm getting really mental Mum
I think I'm going mad
I'm not sure of the time of day
And my life is really bad

Please come and do the washing
I can't stand to look once more at it
The smell is bad, I can't eat in here
Everything's covered in cocky shit

And while you're here you can help me
With the things I've gotta do
Don't answer back. I know I'm right
Why do you create a major coup?

I feel you're getting down on me
I think you're really pissed
But I don't care if you feel that way
Cause I want to be the bitch

Dad, it happened again, she got my goat,
Please tell her of my side
I can't handle all the bullshit
When I'm living to survive

The Base Element

For all of the bullshit, the whoring can stay
I don't know why I do it, is it really the pay?
It's not for the sex or the feel of male sweat
And it's definitely not cos I'm horny and wet
People I take one-on-one now you see?
It's easier. A cop-out? Perhaps, but fuck me!

Penny Fuck

Going so low is lethal
My ad is very cheap
It's not even in my area
I'm meeting some real creeps

I'm going to get off 'action' drugs
I'm going to stick with pot
I'm going to get away from this
Stupid fucking lot

I'll look for a brothel
A small little place
But busy, must be busy
Get me back in the race

A-Ha!

I'm working in a brothel
A clean and quiet place
The girls are good but bitchy
So I try to set my pace

We compete for their attention
The customers I mean
One by one we all go out
And return, grimacing

Everybody's desperate
We badly need to earn
I much preferred being on my own
Than taking fucking turn

Working Life

What is this? An intro?
Oh God I hate this shit
The politics of who wins the job
And then the whispers, "Bitch"

Some hang around, cajoling
Some make it very fast
We all are on our tenterhooks
"Please make this traffic last"

I think they want a female
Who can get down on the floor
Get completely dirty
And smile through it all

Take it now, and take it all
I grimace and oblige
It's all for one and all for me
For both on either side

Tricks of the Trade

"Get off your back and on your knees,
It's better for your bum"
I felt guilty then because I knew
How idle I had been for some

"The main thing is make them happy
Give them what they want
Don't put up with shit but give a bit
Show them what you've got"

No time to work out? Work out on them
Be discreet though if you're worried
Men will believe you look alright
If you don't let on you're bothered

Wake up Call

My pills aren't working

Confusing at least

They worked so well

That I thought that was it

A few years go by

Addiction in place

To these pills that aren't working

And my public face

Is down the plug hole

And out the door

I've been losing the plot

For three years or more

Cycle starts again

I have to keep on working
I'll change the meds for sure
But working suits me like it or not
I'll advertise even more

My thoughts are 'get my meds right'
and find an even balance
Then I will be working even harder
And using my business talents

No

Women are women

And sex workers are too

To work in the industry

I need a view

Perspective that stops me

From feeling raped

I have to know that I am right

Or I'd know that I am bait

It has just meant that I've been used

In every different way

Sometimes I don't know how to act

I feel that I should play

Whenever someone's nice to me

I feel I owe them some

I don't have much to give though, now

Except the tales that I can spin

They only like to hear my tales
Because it reinforces their idea
That I like the image I've created
And I sometimes live in fear.

I'm back

I'm working from my own place now
They come in through the front
I'm not ashamed; nothing to hide
If neighbours ask I'm blunt

The ad is good; the clients great
I'm really pulling in
I look real good from loss in weight
But not everyone likes me thin

For now I've got the flat I want
Paying often and steady rent
I'm earning all the cash I need
And refrain from getting bent

The main point is I'm legal
On my own and very straight
I've got everything I could really want
I don't need a constant mate.

Disordered Workers Life

Bipolar disorder makes this job easy

For me, and a pleasure to do

It helps me to beat the

Illness and teaches me too

First there's the phone calls

My response changes each time

In the early days nothing is sure

I'll work out my line

Then they arrive

Crucial this moment

It determines the drive

Makes it easy to hone it

Intros are different for everyone

And unique for me

Do they reject me,

And curse as they leave?

When I am lucky,
And they stay for the hour
After is hard times
Having cash can turn sour

I used to get manic
Go out and spend
Now I wait longer
And no longer pretend

That it will not affect me
It does and it will
So these days I clean more
Before counting the till

Conviction or Convicted

I found a piece of paper
Hidden in a book
The message was a real one
I took a closer look

The words that Des had written
Deserved an explanation fast
"You are not a man of conviction
You only think you are"

Later on he told me
That it was written to
A temporary mate who'd told him
How his past was true

I think that when I look back
I could say the very same
It's unreasonable to think other
Since I am not so . . . tame

A smart head on young shoulders
Has the desired effect
Of justifying anything
Tomorrow to affect

And affect the situation
Is exactly what we do
When we easily make decisions
And then follow through

Epiphany

I wish I didn't get angry

I wish I didn't get loud

I wish I could say I didn't put up with this shit

Without voicing my concerns out so loud.

The truth is I did get real angry

I lost the plot time and again

But I was raging against the wrong people I think

And it's a bad habit I still attend

The ones who should have been angering me

Were the ones who were sticking it in

But I felt like they understood me

In some bent way, but not like my kin

My mother calls me a pervert

My brother doesn't call me at all

They don't understand; they think that's my fault

Like from my stance I should naturally fall

I just wish I'd been taught so much sooner

Taught respectful, mutual love

Coz I took their mistrust and derision

And gave myself up for a buck.

The Endurance of It

I remember all the people
Who felt I wasn't worth
The effort they had made with me
Their departures made things worse
It wasn't til there was no one left
That I started to get well
But that was just the end result
The path to which was hell
My mental health was always on
The table with my peers
It was always the excuse for
Bad behaviour through the years
But maybe mental illness
For me was just a ruse
I also tried to use it
As a profitable excuse
These days I am wholly sick
Of defining myself that way
I'm sick of acting sick
But it will not go away

My Manifesto

Positivity is the answer
A filter for the pain
Chaotic life or no, my dear
The pain is there the same

Accept the truth, hold on to it
You have a reason to be sad
Let that be a source of strength
Not an excuse for bad

Find a way to build a bridge
Walk across the filthy muck
Don't let people get you down
And give a pleasant fuck.

Epilogue

Abortion

He's leaving me barren, aborted at the source,

He exited prison so healthy, I got pregnant yes of course.

We never used protection, it was silly as all hell,

I've been working my little ass off while he's been in a cell.

I used them with my clients but not in my private life to date

And now my period is due, and it is all too late.

I cannot go through birth, it seems like utter torture

And I wouldn't want to give the bub to Mum, I think she'd hurt her

I cannot have a child like this, living week to week.

Shacked up with a dealer who can't his ends make meet.

I'm using speed while pregnant and yes I am ashamed

But addicted and unmedicated so maybe not to blame.

We've broken up, I mean, obviously, this whole thing's way too bad

And now I'm thinking way too much and I am very
sad

Apology Waiting

Acceptance of an apology
That's all I had to do
The broken man who fronted
For the things he did, he rued
Not long emancipated
Let out of the cell
To come home to loving girlfriend
To find herself she'd sell
I wrapped him in addiction
That I'd continued on
While he was being punished
For his strictly legal wrong
So we'd fought in our drug stupor
We'd yelled and even struck
He's gone out to get some heroin
And now was feeling yuck
So proud of getting clean in jail
But now to see his slut
Carry on and bait him on
He slams the front door shut
And I am left now reeling
It will take years for me to see
How shockingly I treated him
And where that would leave me
Broke, with pregnant belly
No more home to rent

Back with my own parents
My liberty's been spent

Utterly:

A Biography in Verse

The Real Steel

Luck happens, chance is sent
Forever is a moment spent

Take the subject, take the time
Always to include a rhyme

Straighten thoughts and clear the way
There are things I have to say

Send me someone who will hear
Hidden thoughts that aren't quite clear.

In this verse I write each day,
In the ether, in the fray,

I seek something that is real,
The real me beneath the steel

Come upon my wayward lair
Have a listen, take a chair

111

Motivation

I fall into an emotional heap with little provocation
My emotions go from nought to taut from things that
could be taken
In two ways or more, but it is just the obvious
indication
Of some disrespect that's shown to me, that causes
consternation
I want to talk in honesty, and express my situation
But the folks who do the listening are the cause of my
frustration
Everyone's unique and that is not exaggeration
But everybody shares the same selfish inclination
And so do I, there is no doubt, I come with motivation
To tell my side and be received by those with
education
Who know that they are not always right in
application
And can acquiesce or make some other visible
donation
To my self-esteem and my true self-worth
Cos I'm in constant re-creation

Reputation

The accident was the start of it, the unwellness that I
mean
I was behaving most unusually, and my decisions
could be seen
The accident was a head injury I got inside a car
We were driving in the country but not going very far
We hit a truck on a narrow road, just down on the
coast
A coma for some days, then I'd act on innermost
I flew to some decisions I'd been wanting to make a
while
I wanted a boy to talk to me, and give me his sweet
smile
That didn't happen any easier when I finally went
back
The school that I returned to, I totally couldn't hack
So glad I was of starting my adult life at last
I didn't recognise that I was building my future past

Jeunesse

I grew up watching opera. Unbelievable I know

I used to see the symphony play and the experience
did sow

A sense of sophistication, misplaced though I am sure

I thought that I was all of that, just coz I stayed for
more

My peers were watching tv, but we didn't buy the
hype

We didn't have a tv, our family weren't the type

Us kids retired at 7.30 and the temptation wasn't there

To stay up late and listen to the music on the air

AM radio is all we had until the early 90s

And I didn't know any of the music that played so
lamely, nightly

My peers were listening to Kiss, Bon Jovi and
probably AC/DC?

I didn't know of any of it until I bought a CD

We didn't have a player, but I figured we would
sometime

So I bought a bit of music and bided my sweet time

Settlement Betterment

I'd anticipated this moment, waited for the day

The reality of my health concerns came right down to
pay

They ushered me through the doors, I felt the chilly
air

Then seated me at the table, right in the barrister's
chair

I fiddled at the enormous desk while the lawyers
finalised

The offer they said would bring a smile right into my
eyes

Certainly, they had it right, the figure was so welcome

But they gave it to the Public Trust to manage and
accustom

They're renting me a unit with a hundred bucks for
living

But I need clothes and furniture too, and they aren't
really giving

It is a really difficult time; I feel that I've been lied to
It is at this point that I really feel inspired to

Rail at everybody, no matter who they are
Yell at everybody, and roll my brand-new car

80s

I blamed my parents for who knows what

But it came clearer later

I'd not had a well-rounded youth

I was missing social structure

Shopping at Sussan Grae

At 11 years, just youth!

My heart was tearing as we walked

By Dotti or City Surf

I wore Target to the Opera

And that's the best I got

My desires for a flattering line

Were completely blocked

All of my week evenings

Were spent in church youth groups

Girls' brigade or children's choir

I was completely duped

I thought that everyone did this

How strange I did not compute

80s kids owned the streets

But my life at home was mute

Irony of my mind

The compo was appreciated, you have no idea

But it left me with some questions, and I find myself
in fear

Cos the settlement was expected and thoroughly
researched

But my feelings towards the whole ordeal, I will
forever search

The injury changed my personality and in my mind
for better

But that's not the way we played it, in the legal letter

We said I was a victim of a change in circumstance

But that's not entirely true, over my shoulder I often
glance

Yes, I continue to suffer from some kinds of mental
illness

But I think I would regardless, it's an artist's business

Cos the accident was the best thing to happen to me

And the money from the compo caps it wonderfully

Social Woeful

I wasn't really conscious

Of the friends that I had made

I was dependent on attention

But didn't have a firm comrade

There was Becca who I wanted

But I was mystified by the way

And there was Des who couldn't get rid of me

I'd insist and simply stay

There were people who came in and out

I'd satisfy their stories

But I treated them with disregard,

And transgressed their territories

Slow Slide

I got all my money, well the Trust did of course
And I bought that nice car, as in previous post

The first thing I did was offer a ride
To a young guy with cool friends I knew on the side

We drove down to Nimbin for Mardi Gras
We all had a good time, camped in the grass

I met Nick after that weekend and thoroughly grew
Addicted to heroin, which our friends knew

I got really sick and I had to answer
For my behaviour when my car was on fire.

Maybe like six months in, Nick passed away
I'm not really sure what happened that day.

Something about heroin, but by then I was clean
I don't know from that, how much more I can glean

It seems really stupid that I was using the slow

I guess that I had to try, it's my life flow

Forsaken

I'm alone here, all alone, and isolated from the rest
It seems the heroin use meant I thoroughly failed the
test

I was warned that others wouldn't let me enjoy some
cash
I was told they would be at me and want to score
some hash

But they've left me, they're all gone now, and it's clear
that I'm alone
They do not want to know me, my behaviour not
condoned

I'm looking for some contacts, anyone will do
I found this bitch in Ashgrove and her rude and judge-
y crew

Through her I met a man to date but he's really not the
best

I'm still hanging with my ex's son and I prefer him to
the rest

But he doesn't want a serious relationship with me at
all
So I'm leaving him, cos convincing him, I do not need
the call

I'm still hanging with my ex's son and I prefer him to
the rest

Pittance

They give me merely pittance, it's a total tragedy

I have thousands in the bank but the Trust will not let

me see

I cannot have a lavish life, I cannot even shop

They want me to get invoices, they want to mark my

spot

It's crazy! No clothing store is going to accept a

cheque

They treat me with disdain and my countenance is

wrecked

I've had to go do sex work cos it's the job that I do

best

I'm able to buy the expensive things and let the Trust

handle the rest

Autumn Fantasies

Chirpy in the morning

Its crispy in the fall

I want to ring my lover

Who keeps me in enthral

I love to hear his stories

Love to hear his tales

I love to share with him as well

And see his face go pale

We sit together on the couch

I share with him the basics

Of what and who and how I've done

This job that is so crazy

He holds my hand and sees how much

My clients have been a burden

He laughs nervously and then replies

With some kind of learned jargon

He orders me some dinner,

and sets a pleasant tone
Just putting on some music
Makes the whole place feel like home

It is a fantasy of course
As I wake up today
Of the perfect guy that I could have
With whom I'd want to play

Relationships and all that jazz
But I am busy giving
I'm working like a woman
And make a damn good living

Of course, I have my fantasies
My dreams of ever love
I'll do it when I've achieved some things
When I've raised myself above

Rendezvous

The Oxley pub was where we met
He was drinking there with mates
One of them, a friend of mine
I liked to think it fate

His presence struck me instantly
I wanted to talk more
He exuded a warmth and generosity
In spirit and candour

I asked a curious question
And he looked at me with care
I dropped my chin, looked up at him
It was like a subtle dare

We moved our private party
To his house around the corner
We talked for hours about ourselves
My heart was growing warmer

I fell in love about that time

I really don't know why

He was grey, bearded and sort of rough

But his piercing eyes were kind

The Buckage

Buck is very tall, with hair cascading down his back

His body hair is perfect and his stomach's very flat

His legs are long and lean and tan, and with developed calves

His arms are lithe and strong and sure just like his tender heart

He used to work as one of many cooks at Broncos Leagues

But he wasn't working anymore, his back trouble made him leave

He has gorgeous and intelligent adult daughters that I know

And a son he hasn't seen, since he was only one year old

I'm really glad I've met him; he entertains me much

His propensity to talk so well with embellishments and such

I don't know if what he's telling me is true in any sense

But I don't think that it matters when it's just his own 2 cents

Heart Start

For what it's worth I have to say
You have got yourself a friend
Someone who'll always be there
Someone who won't bend

You can trust in me my gorgeous friend
I will not let you down
I will not let you be upset or
Have a grumpy frown

I'll feed you the most delicious food
That you could hope to eat
I'll give you too, nice clothes and shoes
To don upon your feet

I want to give you a special life
In which you can be free
The sort of life I wish someone
Had kindly offered me

Umbilical

I've always had a very

Complex relationship with my folks

I'm attached to them emotionally

I cannot break the yoke

I've been trusting in them implicitly

Since I was a little girl

They didn't see the wild child within

They simply saw white pearl

I followed their instructions

But I was always real irate

Their traditions and their values

I came to totally hate.

Borderline

Let's get one thing sorted

I am a nut

I have a mental illness

And I make a manic fuss

I've tried to play it cool with Buck

I've tried to play along

I've tried to be just what he wants

But I always get it wrong

Anger is not new to me

I can do it too

I can be right in your face

And throw it back at you

But I'm getting broken bones here

I'm not achieving shit

A few months later he moves out

And I can't afford to live

Occasionally, I go and get a job

He handles that quite well

But it feels a little insulting

Like he just wants space to dwell

In his own fucked up little world

Instead of getting the help he needs

Instead of going and improving life

He lets his emotions bleed

Then as soon as I say something

That doesn't fit his mood

The arguments start and goals laid waste

And our relationship is screwed

Diagnoses
I'm officially Schizoaffective with a side of Borderline
PTSD is in there and anxiety all the time

How does it affect me? Well, my mood goes up and
down
But everybody's does so what causes concerned
frown?

The symptoms of my disorder are mania or depression
I find it hard to class myself in the middle of that
progression

So, when I'm "manic", I am moving forward healthy
in my life
That's not the same for everyone but for me it's kind
of nice

That when I'm up, I'm doing well but when I'm down,
oh boy
I'm abusive, violent, crazed indeed, depressed and
hardly coy

There is the head injury, the lack of executive skills

That cause me to go days between showers, or eating
meals

I'm taking medication, I'm getting therapy

And I'm writing and that's the best thing for my
sanity

Requested

I must confess, I've pushed the Trust
To buy me things expensive
I've also wrecked my car at times
To count I'm apprehensive

I ask them for advances
To which I've learned they're predisposed
To handing out quite willingly
For any reason I propose

But it's left me almost broke now
And forever more
I still have my house but in reality
I actually am quite poor

Broken Muse

Too fragile, too manic, too needy, too much
I lost half of my money from all of that stuff

But this latest? Abusive. Abusive and rough
And I didn't deserve it, not one fucking touch

At least for a couple of years, things have improved
Since they altered my medication and calmed down
my mood

So, he pushed even harder, my will that would split
After days of the incredulous bullshit he spit

I lost it. 'It's final, it will end tonight!'
He heard me, but saw me out there in full flight

He drags me to his level, calming only when scored
And I am left broken, a state I abhor

Prayerful

I blast them, I'm always ringing them
On the yellowing Telstra phone
I ring them if I want a fight
Even if I'm not at home

I ring them up for money
I call them up to talk
It is always about me
At my stories they do baulk

I know I'm doing the wrong thing by them
I know I should be careful
They're all I got but I know
They are forever prayerful

They'll let me have my say with them
They'll let me get it out
Although they won't put up with crap
Their love is not in doubt

Cruel Blow

My father's colleague was driving the day I hit my
head
I wound up in the hospital, but I could have turned out
dead
My dad expects me to achieve what I would sans
injury
And my mother screams at me for my idiosyncrasies
I would have thought they'd want their daughter to
live well
Like when I need a bit of milk or just some fucking
help
If they would simply stop complaining and just help
me out a bit
Recognise who I am now, and stop giving me the shits
I know that I have lived my life in a way they
wouldn't choose
But when it's my life I have to live, I've not much left
to lose
I'll take my chances and do the things that help me to
self-grow

And their opinion doesn't matter, when it comes to
what I know

Religious Bitch

Do I have to take up religion so I am not a bitch?

And if it's to be religion, then of them all choose
which?

I grew up in the Christian folds of that it is quite plain

I grew up thinking that for inherent faults I will be
blamed

I don't like feeling that this God who they say loves
me

Is just in fact trying to trick and balderdash me

I want to be a good person but I want it to be real

I want to feel it in my guts, a wholly loving meal

I'm trying to be mindful of the things I do each day

I want to be a good person, without a tithe to pay

To benevolent institutions that are there to inspire
hope

Cos the truth is that they just isolate me from their

trope

Voiceless

Thoughts echo in the silence

I scream into the void

I cannot feel my fingers

And everything is cold

Music, please a pattern

Structure with a beat

I need to move my body

Even in my seat

It's scary when accosted

By a house so very quiet

Where is the life, the energy

The spirit and the vibe?

Do people here not need it?

Or have they not discovered

A genre that will lift them up,

A style that will be wanted?

It makes me feel undesired too

Like my energy's not welcome

I want to leave their boring life

And go where I'm accustomed

Validation

I just want you to see me,

Who I truly am

Why do you look right through me?

Like when I take a stand

When I push for your acceptance,

When I ask you, please, to be,

More polite and yes, more generous,

Your gifts to me are key…

Well, I didn't expect this poem

To go quite just like that,

But it's true that my love language

Is definitely tit-for-tat

I want them to acknowledge

The person I've become

But they don't, so I just ask for things

Just a simple crumb

Rage

There is a lot of rage in me,

A lot of petty spite

It comes from past injustices

It comes out in what I write

I do not mean harm on the ones

Of whom I speak and say

These things that are opinion,

Your fears I would allay

I'm trying to sort out the painful

Ways I've lived my life

Stupid things that I have done,

And who has caused me strife

But I shouldn't attack just anyone

Who comes into my view

As the saying goes, we know so well,

And that is, you do you

Smokers Haunt

I want to have a cigarette,

I want to have a smoke

I want to suck that foul shit down,

Until my lungs, they choke

My lungs are black, or gonna be

My throat will suffer too

My teeth will rot and all fall out

Won't be a pretty view

But there are those around me

Who are starting to feel the results

Of the investment in their deaths,

And I share their faults

The solution? None. I'm not ready yet,

Not ready to quit the smoke

It's a part of who I am these days,

Especially the occasional toke

Maybe when I quit the pot,

I'll quit the smokes as well

Maybe, maybe. It's all far off

A story to maybe tell

Milton Hilton

For what it's worth I'm thinking,

Maybe we should be friends

I'm not real keen on walking, when

We've achieved these timely ends

With the people who have hurt us,

The people who didn't care

They threw us in a ward of pain,

And in it left us there

You saw me when I came in,

I was angry and upset

You cast your eyes upon me,

And saw all the neglect

We share a history without a past

We understand the pain

The hurt and the depression

Which are not quite of the same

The hurt is because we love ourselves

The depression makes no sense
It fills us with a numbing feel,
But the pains somewhat intense

You shared with me like no one else
When I was lost in fear
I shared with you, and we both grew,
And came to shed a tear

A tear of rehabilitation,
A tear of self-respect
An acknowledgement we would prevail,
A truth to self-reflect

So now we are quite stable,
And we forgive ourselves as well,
For the pain that others caused us,
That no one wants hear tell

I want you in my life, my friend,
I want you to be here
I want to shield you from the storm,

And you me, from what I fear

151

Not Charlotte Brontë

Everywhere I go, I'm told that I am not ok

Not because of things I do, more for what I say

Everybody's traumatised, but no one wants to listen

Noone wants to know the pain that in others they have

bidden

There are certain groups of people who cause me to

seek hell

But I can't say who or what they do, that makes me

want to yell

Not if I'm a part of the community as a whole

I've got to play the game and not my pain extol

It isn't any different than Charlotte Brontë's day

We've images to uphold and values to obey

Advice for Borderlines

The best advice I ever got was "Shut up and fuck off"

T'was my lover Buck who told me, and yes he was quite gruff

For years and years, I'd carried on and couldn't give a toss

Now this man I loved so much, told me, nuff's enough

My mood settled dramatically, I got into a groove

My medication fit my needs and I stopped being so rude

My lover took a little time to acclimatise and sync

He had to learn to quell his tongue and rages now I think

We managed to get through the first few years of strong abuse

But when I got home from hospital, I set my demons loose

I mean I let them go you see, I didn't keep them on

I let them go and kept my love, this gruff and surly man

Union

We'd leave on Thursday, payday, and walk to get
some chips
He'd saunter gently with his bag rocking against his
hips

Then we'd head for Indro, to the pub for him to sit
Quietly and sip a beer, while I went to get our shit

It was a routine for us, that we practised fortnightly
But for half the time I had a car, which came in
handily

We didn't spend our nights together, he would sit and
watch TV
I would be happy with my tunes, to him frustratingly

But we had a solid friendship, a love that we did share
And nobody could compete with his kindness and his
care

Diagnosis

He let me call the ambulance

He struggled to breathe or walk

His feet were swollen three times the size

And he could barely talk

I called his daughter when he left

To tell her where to go

I got there an hour later

So all of us would know

It turns out that one lung is black

And that he needs a stent

We could have lost him at that time

He could've turned out dead

Later the chemotherapy

Got him pretty bad

He ended up with a chest infection

And put back into the ward

Second time he cheated death

Is what the doctor said

It was just a question then

Of where he'd lay his head

Deadly Requests

He asks for things that are dangerous

Begs the questions that are serious

Pushes his mortality

Breathes in his fatality

Like it's nothing, like it doesn't matter

It does matter… but to who?

If I were him, I'd smoke and drink,

I'd shoot up smack, not take a hint

So, I'm comfortable with his own decisions

Even if they contravene some wisdom

But he needs to be comfortable with mine

I cannot be his all the time

He needs a carer and I can't do it

I can't even manage my own shit

I have a mental illness, that is me

My attitude is completely free

But should my life be free

Of responsibility?

Ever love

A relief, a dreaded, disgusting relief
A feeling of peace though knowledge of grief
Well, I'm hoping so anyway, it's feeling all wrong
The mania threatens, it's coming on strong

I want to be there right to the end
He needs to know that I'm always his friend
But he makes it so hard, so demanding and rude
Belligerent the word, attitude he exudes

His family are watching, they're not sure I can do it
But in dire straits I've stepped up, even run up when
needed
I've had much support; all want to be sure
That he's happy and rested and ready for more

More of the chemo, or more of the drugs
More of the visits from family with hugs
His children love him and they appreciate me
That's all I would ask for he allows me to be free

I do what I can, I love him to death
I wish I could offer him much better health
He wants to be home and pass away here
That is not something that I overly fear

If there's one thing to be learned, I'm probably
missing it
I'm just trying hard to get up and deal with it
That and my own issues, who wants to know?
My priority should be Buckley, not on my flow

Friendsly

I have a friend, well, he's really Bucks
But he's been standing by us both
So-called friends have let us down
But it's like Marcus took an oath
My parents are here and present
Ready to do their best
Mum organised a wheelchair
Dads helping with the rest
Buck hasn't been surrounded by
A throng of eager friends
But the ones we've got are faithful
And do not seek own ends
My support worker comes to see
Buck in his hospital room
And when he needs me, I am there
On my way and soon
So, we're lucky, he's not alone
Of that, I make quite sure
His children have rallied all around
That's what family's for

Pain
A relief, a dreaded disgusting relief?
Fuck no! Not feeling it, not fucking now

Buck went just a week ago
Gasping the how

I came home to find him
Prostrate on the couch

His arms were behind him, and
Open his mouth

Every so often
He would inhale

Screaming, I clutched at him
As he grew more pale

I had the ambulance
There on the phone

They told me to compress his chest
While still alone

The medics got here
Pretty damn quick

But it made no difference
He had been picked

Out from the life force and
Into the heavens

We're all just hoping
He went with the sevens…

Recovery

Forgetting all the difficulties that I have overcome

Accepting the successes that are yet to come

I cling to what will cause inspiration to revive

A poem, like a jingle or a little jive

I want to move past the point where my inner pain is
key

I want to start writing more with Positivity

The speaker's set to music and I miserably spend

My time listening to music while with my thoughts I
must contend

Stewing in It

What am I to make of it?

What am I to do?

I'm grieving and alone here

But in my grief, I cannot stew

I was working while he was alive

Whoring. On the job

Now I'm just lying around here

Lonely and a slob

It's not the ideal way to be

Or path that I could choose

I think I'll go back to working

Before my sanity I lose

Superficial

Superficial is the reason, is the order for today

I'm troubled by things greatly, and don't want those

things to stay

I want to get on top of what is happening in my head

I want to work out what it is that's necessarily said

I'm going to focus on my health and helping others

too

Not be selfish and demanding and do things I will rue

I can be superficial and still try to hold a place

Of love and understanding, peace, angelic grace

Disappointment and Uncertainty

Disappointment and uncertainty are the words that
spring to mind
I'm standing on the top step of this unit, hard to find
I gather my coat around me, knock upon the door
A voice inside alerts me, that yes, I have been heard

The moon was not far up yet, it was early in the night
The wind picked up and a siren blared, giving me a
fright
Suddenly the door opened and my client stood there
staring
A bearded man with shaggy hair, beer in hand, he's
leering

He's scratching his ass while assessing me, checking
out my figure
He's naturally skinny and I admit I'm somewhat
bigger
I can tell that he is wondering if it was worth the
while

Of ringing a professional girl who comes out with this
style
Over forty and overweight, I work for every dollar
I wish I'd had the confidence when I was so much
younger
He decides not to waste his Viagra and invites me to
come in
It's not much for that I grant you, but it's definitely a
win

Steel

They say I have to fuck them
Fuck them with my mind
To tell the truth I'm not that type
That's not my way defined

I treat them like a hook up
I'm friendly and relaxed
I don't tell them my life story
But I anticipate a match

With many of my clients
Coz they're looking for something real
In this superficial world we live in
Where they have to be like steel

I treat them very warmly
Like a girl who's always been
A friend of their favourite sister
And everything that means

It's like I am the girlfriend

Of a hundred different guys

And it's so easy cos I'm not playing

I'm not trying to disguise

Let Me Be

I do this for a reason, I have a goal you see
It don't make sense to everyone, but it makes sense to
me

I want to live an artistic life, independent of chagrin
But it is hard when most don't know how to even
begin

I take the money from the men who come to see and
do
But channel my own energies into mental things to
chew

Poems or some paintings are my real reason to be
I design my life to suit my tastes, and then invite them
all to tea

But the clients they don't want that, and my friends
are rare and few
I wish to find a niche in life, but I'm driven to argue

About the ethics of my job, and the worth of what I
make
I wish that people could step back a bit, and think
before they take

Exception to the way I live, and what it means to them
I'm trying to become my own, not just be for the men

I'm happy with the life I've made, but it is perplexing
me to see
That people are so threatened by my choice to just be
me

Jam Jar

Windchime in the window
Jam jar on the sill
I eat my breakfast quietly
While she counts up the till

It was profitable for us last night
It was money in the bank
We had these two old lawyers
Loaded though they stank

We entertained them all the night
And charged for everything
One of them happened to have
A pretty diamond ring

We got that off him, me and Jill
We were working here last night
This little brothel in the 'burbs
Where we stay out of sight

But now it's morn, I'm tired and had

Enough of all the talking
I just want to get my pay then
To my car I will be walking.

Plenty of Hooks

Dating as a sex worker, do I tell the truth?
Cos every time these assholes start to act uncouth

Thinking that I'm free, and happy to oblige
Thinking cos I'm on a dating app, I want to body slide

I shouldn't be so open; I have no fucking shame
I use unmade up face and even state my own first
name

It's cos I am retired now, or sort of, it depends
On what dating app I'm using, to achieve what kind of
ends

I have to be most careful but still true to my values
Of living strong and honestly but not being hurt or
abused

I think I might be as unique as anyone is in this world
Cos I really just don't care and I'm not afraid of
getting old

Musings

While wandering through life I be

Troubled by the complexity

Should be so easy, is a farce

A playful game of steal the heart

It seems so simple, not the truth

So many out there are uncouth

I seek support now, that is true

More than superficial you

I'm mindful of my choices

I'm weighing up the odds

Do I spend like summer's coming?

Or stick to the goal and job?

Cos I really want to do

So many things at once

I want to save and I want to spend,

But to spend, I'd be a chump

I have to stick to waiting

For the goals to come to be

For reality to match the hope

That this person could be me

Trauma Stormer

The table's strewn with dumpers, and it's really such a
shame
Cos there is no mistaking, that I'm the one to blame

I smoke so many cigarettes, I'm pushing forty on most
days
And the air in my small unit, is always such a haze

I'd like to quit, I think I would, smoking killed my
friend
That was ten long years ago, and the hurting never
ends

It affected me quite deeply, and I gave up for a time
But I took it up again, when I had been fed a scary
line

I was raped, you see, and cut off from my family for a
while
The experience fills me now with so much fuckin'
bile

I got a tattoo on my wrist of Dignity, a joke!
When I look at how I live my life and what I have
since wrote

It might be just a reminder of what I should do next
But it feels a constant reminder of that serial sex pest

But how does this relate to smoking, I really do not
know
I suppose it's my decision of how I'd like to go

But it's really not! I remember how hard it was to see
Him suffocating on the floor, while I screamed out,
"Fucking breathe!!"

Animosity

I let them take liberties

Transgress parts of me

I justify it isn't hurting

But my instinct pulls me away

Inwardly, I am living a whole different life

Than the one I'm playing

A role but living honestly

Honesty in untruthfulness

Who am I lying to?

Not taking account my animosity

Their opinion matters more than my own desires

And I cannot satisfy either

Orgasm

Please don't make me orgasm, I whisper to myself
It's futile though cos every man wants that for himself

He wants to take you higher, lift you to the skies
But it just feels like he's skinning me, skinning me
alive

Removing organs consciously and without an
anaesthetic
That's what being forced to cum feels like to an addict

I really didn't want this and I asked you not to go
To these depths that you are taking me, they're not
heights, they're so low

Conclusion

It's frustrating when I write a poem deep into the night
And I cannot tell someone about it till the morning
light

About an hour post penning it, I go back to see
What it is I've written and what it means for me

Regularly revelations, things are brought to bear
Brought to my attention, and brung up for some air

I learn things about my friends and what it means to
do
The things we love with whom we care and how we
somehow grew

I'm working through my trauma, simply by writing
verse
I'm learning about my pain and it's not getting any
worse

I'm remembering, I'm dealing with it, I'm sharing with
my shrink
And together we work out what it is, I'm supposed to
think

It's good me writing poetry, I'm learning about myself
I'm coming to an understanding, it simply can't be
helped

Insight

Thinking I'm through with working
In the global sex trade

I loved my time while doing it
I don't think I was afraid

But I'm looking for some meaning
Of depths, new paths to tread

I want to become who I need
For me, just me instead

Of giving to these assholes
Loving boyfriends too, of course

I've been shouting into the ether
Until I'm fucking hoarse

Looking for some meaning
I think that it's within

I need to love myself now

As my mother did intend

Unsettled Thoughts

I have been very lucky, but the people around me
weren't
I wonder if that's coincidence, or if it's something
worse

It might be said, I suck on the life, of everyone I meet
Their experiences and perspectives, I'll completely eat

I'll take all of the goodness, and leave them, with
some zest
Leave them really knowing that they completely
failed the test

I hope that Buck was happy. I hope I didn't hurt Nick.
I hope my parents forgive me for being a drug
addicted bitch.

I'm doing ok but should I feel guilty at my position?
Cos I didn't get here by myself and I had a lousy
disposition

All I can do is look forward to what is yet to come

And hope that what has come before leaves a positive,

loving sum

Trying hands

We have been dealt with some bad hands

Bad hands throughout the years

I've lived through those tense moments

And I've definitely shed some tears

For Buck, my friend, I've had to live,

Had to live through death

I've grieved and I've lamented loss

Knelt down to feel his breath

At work, my rash decision making

Placed me in the care

Of men who did not recognise

The goodness that I shared

The clients got the best of me

My positive pleasing sense

And my friends and family had to bear

The brunt of all the rest

All along I made an effort

To improve in some small way

Proactive like my father taught me

No day quite like today

Dedication

Dad, I've always been impressed with how you live
your life
Your discipline astounds me and the way you love
your wife

As your daughter, I have learned so much about the
things that count
About going for your goal and never putting on a pout

You know what is important and you know who will
be true
And knowing you my father, what is true is you

You're clear in your intentions, your boundaries are in
place
You have a healthy outlook and always a smiling face

I'm so impressed by you, your discipline and your
skills
You've given us opportunities that I experienced with
thrill

Like opera and live music, you brought it home to
share
And took us to sweet places, like season tickets to the
fair

I thank you for the interest you have paid into my
prose
And the poetry too, you encouraged me when others
didn't know

Lessons

What lessons can I derive from my experiences thus
far?
I have not become successful, not yet become a star

I have worked a little here and there, and
contemplated life
I have had some awful luck, and I definitely had some
strife

I've lost two boys, and gained a disabled pension plan
But I've gotten through years of working without
needing a medical scan

I have worked on my troubled relationship with my
folks
We have achieved a lot together of that I surely spoke

So, what have I really learned in all this conflict and
misery
That it doesn't feel all woeful, I'm not a victim of
tragedy

Coy Candour

Part One

Profession Obsession

Sex work, a Profession
It directly leaves impressions
To do, to say, to think, to be
To them an indiscretion

They think we do the same things
As each and one another
But cower in confusion when we
Insist they use a rubber

Like that is something unusual
Something ill defined
You're dreaming mate, your culture is
Coarse and unrefined

They think we all have long hair
Big Boobs and Pleaser heels
They think we all have boyfriends
Who cheat and from us steal

What they think would say a lot
If they were honest in their head
But they don't even acknowledge
That it's just what they have read

Amongst their friends they're oh so tough
That image falls away
When the door is opened and now, they're here
Of course they want to play

Uncontrive

Quite a living you are having

You don't take things in half shots!

Looking quizzically, I asked him,

D'ya mean like vodka on the rocks?

Perplexed, then breaks out laughing

His friend is not impressed

But he's not likely to be, anyway

As I often wear a dress

Artless, he accused, and would

Not look me in the eye

I felt the condescension hit me

Like arrows on the fly

I stumbled homeward somehow

But I felt that I'd been seen

But I didn't know of what he saw

Or what artless seemed to mean

A doubt it germinated in

My soul but it came with

An acknowledgement of artistry

In ignorant type bliss

Began begotten

I don't think I knew what the danger was
I don't think that I even cared
I went out, to get some of what, all of
My friends they had already shared

So, my partners were all of these old guys
Who wouldn't go taking me home
After playing the game somewhat badly
They'd force me to get home alone

They left me when they were deflated
Their energy was totally spent
So, tomorrow I'd see my big gay friend
And sit around getting full bent

Convinced to choose prostitution
Like a choice that would make some more sense
To fire my ethical metal
Though young, I developed the rest

Intent

Many are pleasant, many are kind

They usually show up if they're going to, on time

Their intentions are simple

They don't want for much

Just someone to talk to and

Someone to touch

It isn't important to mess with their heads

Cos they're not complicated,

Not when its sex

They all have unique ways

To be satisfied

Cos, they know that in our time,

There's no need to lie

I like these guys, most of them

In their own way

They share vulnerability

Although they do pay

It's a tight rope we're walking

Not touching the floor

The reality, the basics

Of just wanting more

Motherfucking Me

My boyfriend has a problem with the things I do to earn
I do not listen to him anyway, cos I have cash to burn
He doesn't make as much or nearly half of what I do
And he bitches about the pain he's in, to his misogynistic crew
The pain he's ins debatable cos I treat him fucking well
The things I do for him and his are all a fucking tell
They speak the truth of how kind I am, and the things that matter most
Cos I give him so much better than the guys I fucking host
He can keep his bellyaching for his therapist and leave
The business of making money to motherfucking me.

Sketch

The image of a form of you

A gesture or a look

I just don't want to put all of

Your personality in my book

'Tis enough I draw a sketch of you

An image represents

The kind of role you play

And what your deeds have meant

I don't carry a burning flame

I know they do get smothered

The expectations, perceived roles

Of always one another

Fatiguing, it is tiring

I can only take so much

So I keep it on the physical

And its only flesh you touch

Divine, Consign

Cool air, it hits her temple, as
She walks through sliding doors
She's walking out her tension
Shopping, her first amour

The lighting in the store befits
A luxury pantomime
The ladies feeling wicked for
Seeking out a style divine

Her hand rests on her belly
As she contemplates and looks
Should she focus on the fashion,
Or buy lots of lovely books?

She steps a little further in,
In the past, she would be helped
Nowadays the young assistants
Do not care for health nor wealth

She decides against conversing

She quickly walks away

From these shitheads with their mobiles

And all the games they play

They see her as she's leaving

And tossing back her hair

Her demeanour may be fleeting

But it causes them to stare

Part Two

Dignity

The worst part of working
At this job to date
Is the look on people's faces
When they see I'm overweight

A plain and cuddly girl like me
You wouldn't think could do it
You might even make presumptions
That I'll people-please, then rue it

It is, to me, important
To believe in something true
Not the vision that I saw
Or how it affected you

I had to have a certain faith
In my inherent worth
Find something real about me
That for once I do not curse

I'm glad I walked the lonely path

Of decisions, some regrets

I would gladly do it over

If I didn't have a bed

My self-esteem is not for sale

Regardless of my job

I still get the sullen looks, but

My dignity they can't rob

Turn

I wish I had the ability
To write like I could work

To simply make a decision
Place an ad and learn to twerk

I miss the wicked pleasures
Of setting up a space

Writing a catchy intro
Doing up my pretty face

Waiting for the clients
Who want to know my rates

Even though all of the details
Are on my own ad space

Then I get a good one
He's done this all before

Texts an introduction

And doesn't ask for more

The industry's so easy

It's so quick to make a buck

If I want to be a writer

I'll need a lot of luck

Intrepid

Allow me to ejaculate
With this raw word I'll escalate
The opinions that I hold inside
That do concern, definitely divide

I do not think that I was born
To work a living, like some sheep shorn
I'm lucky that I have a way
To fill my time, to work the day

In art and study, I am there
The feeling of success, Beware!
I passed one subject, now do two
I'm going to do a Bachelor's too

I wanted this from childhood since
I'm going to of my life to rinse
The people who would cause me shame
I will not talk to them again

I will deter their petty flow

Their bodies spent can now just go

Pleasure and Pain

Have you ever felt a pleasure

That was intense, like of a pain?

A sudden stimulation

That you went back for, and again

You feel the magic bullet

Like metal, it's a core

Of the part that is erected

That when touched, it feels so sore

The clients, when they reach me

Get me in this way

I cry out in simulation

Of pleasure, cos they pay

But it feels they're going too far

It feels like an assault

I have to take control here

Their energies to halt

I didn't come into this room

To be manhandled and abused

From now this client's number

Is blocked, his jobs refused

Moyster

The pearl of hidden wisdom
In the deep blue sea, a shell
There's a creature in there somewhere
But doesn't like being held

She grows the orb within her
While the flesh inside her swells
Her style is a refined one
But men know not what she held

They want the inner wisdom
But they know not of the pearl
They think the truth that's spoke of
Is in the warm flesh that unfurls

So, the pearl of wisdom's hidden
Until the right one comes along
Who knows how to shuck the oyster
And how to sing the song

Tool

The penis is a tool

That's horribly designed

The owner of it wants it to

Be ready all the time

But it's not, or it is fickle

Very temperamental

One hard minute it's all let's go

And the next? No elemental

He swats it and manhandles

He tries to flog it up

But the girl that's lying next to him

Is getting too fed up

The mood is gone and is replaced

By desperate male shame

Attempting bravado he will try,

But cannot play the game

Part Three

Bolt

I've learned that I cannot depend
On others for my care
I have to walk this life alone
Forever if I dare

It would be nice to have a friend
Someone to walk with
But I do not know where these strange folk
Work, associate, love, or live

I write a poem, read a book
Take a chance and have a look
But I do not know the rules out here
I'll make mistakes, of that I fear

I cannot be a laughingstock
I cannot leave this house unlocked
I want to leave, I want to live
I want to, of this heart, to give

I'd like to love a cherished friend
I will adapt, my will, will bend
Do you have what I might need?
A friendship grown, potential seed?

Please just try to give a fuck
I have only my bitter luck
That saw me withdraw into those
Suburbs anon, the neutral clothes

I want to live, break free and be
A vivid type of personality
I wish I could appeal some more
I wish I knew what it was for

Why do I exist at all?

Care

The fabric tears not gently
The seams will pull away
Costume of a character
Of a previous long day

Sheer cloth that did not nearly hide
The form that lay beneath
The flesh confessed a pressing need
Now relies on self-belief

To turn to other textures
Be elegant, demure
To not reveal the flesh but seek
Clothing that will cure

Crafting her own image
Styling the right tone
Wrapped within an aura
A warmth like from one's home

Bravado

The people who are scared of this
We do not notice, do not miss
They exist in another realm
The things we do would overwhelm
Notice how I think of me
Whenever I refer to we
It is my perspective here to take
What others feel for my own sake
I'm probably wrong but they are too
Your view belongs to only you

Swells and Dips

The ethics and integrity
Attempts to still the ship

To guide a path through storms and all
The currents and the rips

My ego and identity
Separate though conjoined

Work together to then weather, and
Not to let storms then destroy

We must form a set of boundaries
We will build some solid walls

Not let the bastards steal from us
And leave us both appalled

We have only this wooden boat
With place for each one who

Wants to search perimeters
Wants to live and do

The sharks of doubts surrounding
This boat upon the waves

Will not be feared or dwelt upon
Because our resolution stays

We begin our future here on top
Of very little known

The ocean deep will pull at us
Make us want to turn back home

There is no home; it's gone now, said
The captain at the wheel

The quiet determined character
In this metaphorical spiel

The captain is the stubborn will

He will not turn the ship

He'll continue on, and lead us to

A preferable friendship

Niece 1:

Living is a state of mind
An attitude you take

Knowing you can do it all
Just for its own sake

There is no one controlling you
If you just let it go

Discard the expectations
And go on with a flow

The things that hold you back are just
The things you bring around

The people who you love will need
To let you stand your ground

Maybe it's a sudden shift
Maybe much more slow

In order to create something
That you'll be proud to show
I wish for you the luck you need
But the courage that I speak

Is perhaps a little misguided
Cos it can get very bleak

I urge you to consider
Not to do it like I did

Maybe while you work on it
You should keep it under lid

In any case, you have the choice
To take it in the hand

Be a major player and
Make a bold, defiant stand

Part Four

Academic Aspiration

I'd really like to study

Delve into the past

I want to know who thought of it

And how long did it last

I want to examine relationships

People from before

How they went about

Expressing their amour

I'll have to learn of battles

That's all part of it

The women who may inspire the fight

And the men who do conflict

The fashion of the times will tell

More of trade and tribute

The designers and the merchants

Who bring it and contribute

I'm interested in the writing

What has come before,

The parchment tells us one view

Archaeology says much more

I just need to get a picture

A firm and real hold

Of the community that I live in

Within which I try to mould

A more realistic perspective

Of what is expected of me

And then I can find comfort

In acting uniquely

Rose vs Prose

Why is that the poem

That says love's like a rose

Is better in describing feeling

Than how the fresh daisy grows?

Maybe that's opinion

I certainly don't agree

I feel much more peace and joy

When my hands are clean and free

The rose and love that is referred

Is said to be quite deep

But why is it just the reality of

The investment that's so steep?

When I think of love and lovers

And it's likened to a rose

Then I am drawn to see the thorn

And the pain that with it goes

Is it deeper to be unhappy?

Is it superficial to be glad?

To feel the sunshine on you

And know you've not been had?

It's harder to be happy

And for that I think it's worth,

The title of profundity

In the poetry and verse

Time Rhyme

I'm touching on the deficits
Struggle all the time
The words are there but twisted
They don't want to hear my rhyme

They're teaching things I've heard of
Things I ought to know
But it's not what I am needing
It's not helping with the flow

I want to study literature
I really want to explore
Why these pages move me
Why I look for more

I'd like to study everything
Learn in my own way
But it doesn't work just like that
Uni teaches and I pay

Some of my opinions

I realise are for nought

They will not help achieve

The vision that I sought

So I'm finding it confronting

I'm finding it way too hard

Maybe I'll go back to being

An uneducated bard.

Playbook

Did you ever have a feeling?

Did you know you were going to write

a book?, or did it come to you

On a dark and stormy night?

I knew I was artistic, but I felt my art was shit

I knew I had to live, to create meaning out of this

Perhaps it was philosophy

That I was more drawn to

The exciting stretching tentacles

Of minds eyes, what they view

I actually knew I'd be alright and come into some cash

And this was couple of years before I had my head on

crash

I thought I'd be the lover or have lovers of my own

Spilling out from every corner of the world in which I

roam

But no, I didn't feel I knew what I really wanted to say

I just hoped for an exciting life, and my own

philosophy to play

Lit

Every decade gets better
The older I go
The more I am capable
The more that I know

I wouldn't have wanted
To miss out on youth
But I'm glad that it's over
And I'm now long in the tooth

The adventures I undertook
Kept me insane
I really would not want
To go through it again

I've burned in the fire
But now I arise
A poet, a phoenix
Flame lit up inside

Fatigue Float

The world, it isn't talking
It is feeling somewhat black
The visions are not coming
I'm feeling kind of slack

To inspire and prick the senses
To get back to what I know
To express disinhibition
To write with a sure flow

The ideas, they are not lining up
I don't always feel inspired
In the morning after concert
I am feeling somewhat tired

Not in limbs but in thought patterns
I was glowing from my talk
I do not always know the lesson
That I am being taught

It's a lifestyle of a poet

An artistic reverie

Of being home and feeling, waiting,

For a prompt that can then be

A poem or reflection

A wisdom there beheld

That I didn't know I knew of

And now it's out and spelled

The mysterious reception

When I read what I have wrote

Oh, I want it ever-present

I want to always float

a, b, c

a

What do I do with the guilt that I feel so?

Where do I lay down the load?

The cross that I carry is personal

With my conscience I walk memory's road

I wish I could go back and change some things

I'm seeking a salve for my sins

The knowledge of things that I did then

And those that I did offend

Perhaps in the honest reflection

I will finally come to a peace

When agonising my faults I am done with

When in a future, I can believe

b

But really, will it ever be over?

The worry, the stress, and the pain

The transgressions and errors I fall into

Behaviour that seems always the same

I cannot escape from this person,

Her instincts and character flaws

I am beholden to her apprehensions

But also her mission at core

To rely on a vision of pleasure

To construct one's own virtue ideal

Not to wallow in tempting depression

But to find something inside that's more real

Who could hope for a better solution

Than to find it was worth all the pain

And the joy that I feel is encompassing

Will hit no one quite like me the same

c

I hope that in things that I write here

That I'm finally making a point

I hope to give you some hope though

That its worth more than stories and joints

You are creating a past for yourself now

So find something to look back and say

Yeah I really enjoyed my time doing that

Even though I didn't earn any pay

Because life is here for the taking

And you don't have to be happy and glad

But you also can read a good book now

Even though you may feel somewhat sad

I encourage you to think it over

To give living aloud a good go

Cos the time it will move even swifter

And it's gone before you even know.

Part Five

2025

We do not know if we can say
The things that ought be said
We cannot post online the things
We think in our own head

The cameras are watching
The microphone is on
The things we think appear on our
Social media on their own

Everybody's lonely
But no one wants to say
That it's ok to come on over
That, yes, they want to play

The anxiety is palpable
And mixed with depths of rage
The older that I get I see
It's not just up to age

The people who are in power
They watch all this and dare,
The people, us! to question them
We wonder if they care

They set the tone, they mark the price
That we all have to pay
And if someone ends up locked in jail
There's not much we can say

Age

Figures that don't tell the truth

Their faces are a lie

The images they emulate

Are sometimes very dire

The palette displays many sorts

Of textures and of tones

But it is just a coloured wash

Over decaying bones

They're dying, getting older

They're not meaning what they say

They're just trying to get through this

Ere their eternal beds to lay

Reality

Reality, it does not exist

Except in minds that experience this

The thoughts, impressions, and the hate

Determine partly of our fate

What we think begins anew

What they think it's not of you

They're thinking of themselves at first

But do not wish on you the worst

They do not care, they think they do

Remember now, it's up to you

Layers

Like the layers of an onion

The search for inner core

The layers of perception peeled

But intact they tell much more

The skin that is discarded

In the therapeutic way

Rips apart the girl's impressions

Disregarding what will stay

The juicy flesh that makes up part

Of her views which are beheld

Her selective inner vision

The juicy tales it tells

To seek an inner core seems like

Where the truth will lie

But it's in layers of perception

That define the days gone by

Weight of Fate

The quiet administration that goes on behind closed
doors
No one wants to let them know the whys and the
wherefores
My poetry it sings at times, its deceptively divine
But when I go to put together the story, to refine
I am burdened by the weight of the dire capacity
Of my strength but all the weaknesses, the harsh
reality
The truth must be created, I must choose a story in
The examples in the rhythm of the living in the sin
Its exciting, overwhelming, I can be whoever I want
The poems though reality, are manipulated and a front
A story that is memoir will always slant the tale
And I guess that I am as guilty of the flex and the
regale
It's just weird I take reality, and raw emotional weight
And create a different history and an alternative future
fate.

Integrity

The answers to your questions

You have to find within

The truth is for the seeking

And first you must begin

Take a different attitude

To the things that they propose

Choose the most appropriate thing

Before resentment grows

They want you to abide by

The conventions that are in place

But you've got to be at one with

What you see in your own face

You've got to find a niche or nook

In which to invest time

Passion too and discipline

So your creations do align

Examine your own morals

From whence did they arrive?

Are you sure that they are what you need

To make your bright light shine?

You do not have to be the same

As everyone before

You do not have to feel a guilt,

Or shame, you can ignore

Be your own creation

Style your health yourself

Embrace the inner anxiety

Say it how you felt

Be true, build an integrity

Always pay back debts

Build a personality

That no one can upset

Souls Afloat

They're floating through the atmosphere
But coming through her veins
They're here to feel the music
Cos the magic does remain

She opens up her mind and lets
The past in her ferment
And the people who live through her
Can embrace and not lament

They see through her physicality
They experience the now
They're amazed at all the women
Wearing pants, machines that plough

The screens remain a mystery
Will not to them make sense
But the music and the visions are
Both full and most intense

They welcome the conduit for

Them, spirits in the air

They appreciate the visions of

The fashions and the flair

She'll stay in this flow moment,

And perhaps will never leave

She is the raw transmittance

And through her, they can breathe

Part Six

Chappy

Cheerily he chuckles

And pulls on a long lobe

His eyes they are a-twinkling

As he sees his wife disrobe

He never really grew up,

Although his nose grew large

He's balding and gone grey now

His muscles are not hard

But he loves his wife and cherishes

The time she spends to flirt

With an old dog like her husband

Who just loves a bit of skirt

Violet Light

Violet cascading

Streaming down from the sky

The beauty and majesty

Of all up on high

How could you fail

To believe in a god

Who would give us this vision

The trees and the wood

But it's not only vision

That encapsulates time

The sound of the birds and

The musical rhyme

Sensations of walking

Bare foot in the grass

The droplets of dew

The wind while it passed

It lifts up goose pimples

On my bare arms

My scalp it is tickling

This moment will last

Thank God for this image

The sounds and the touch

I'm feeling exhilarated

I'm feeling His love

The End

They die, they do not want to

Their oxygen is cut off

Their voices suffocated

Squeeze out their final cough

No longer to endure the pain

No longer strapped in beds

While deathly howls fill the ward

Crying out in their distress

The home for these old gentlefolk

Is theirs unto the end

Most of them don't even know

How it all began

Horrifying morbidity

Stink, decay and death

The mortifying reality

Of end of life, last breath

Sanctuary

The house it stood there proudly
While the wind whipped up the leaves
The autumnal shades are speaking
Of weather's tiredness, how she grieves
The shingles on the roof appear
To be a part of rusted vision
A fatigue and a weariness
The need to make decisions
The weathered beams that make up all
The walls and verandas round
Are painted in a conducive shade
An orange sort of brown
This countryside is beautiful
Especially days like these
While autumn sun is setting
And there's a slightly chiller breeze

Oh No, an Emo!

Oh God you must be kidding!

An emo! Tell me no

I can't believe you're with him!

He has piercings in his nose

Violet hair, excited

But his mood is much repressed

He writes verse but it is maudlin

And he wears a dress!

Do you loan him all your lipstick?

Does he share your eye make-up?

Dear Lord, I can't get over

How my daughter has fucked up

With a punk! 'No, he's an emo'

Does it even really matter?

Daughter, listen when I tell you

That he's going to get fatter

In his older years he'll grow out of

The style you think is cool

And he'll try to be still relevant

When really, he's a tool

An End

Eluding her eyes, averting
Looking to the side
He watches as the raindrops
Fall from the umbrella, glide

Looking down in guilt he sees
Her feet are clad in boots
Standing in a puddle
He doesn't think; he seems aloof

He wants to turn his back on her
Turn and walk away
But he can feel her eyes upon him
And he knows he's not OK

Putting one hand in his pants
Eager for distraction
He finds a ticket in his pocket
And thinks of taking action

He braves himself to look at her
To gauge what she is thinking
He sees that she's still holding hope
And dismayed his mood starts sinking

I got to go, he mumbles
And she raises an eyebrow
I guess I'll see you next time
That's if you'll allow

She doesn't answer and he turns
And walks quickly away
He doesn't want her to see his tears
Or the pain he tries to allay

She watches him get smaller
And in her mind, she thinks
It's sad to see him angry
But worse when his mood sinks

Sighing, she will gather
Her thoughts and actions to

Get home and out of this rain
This relationship she will rue

Ten To Go

10 the eyes narrow

9 they see the clock

8 he grabs the handles

7 chassis rock

6 he breathes in deeply

5 a strong exhale

4 sounds are forgotten

3 foot on the rail

2 he revs the engine

1 it's now or not

Green the light is go now

Fuck this engine's hot

Psychosis.

I'm kicking goals, I'm hitting targets, I'm surpassing
KPIs.
I have started to market product and I have my inner
drive
If it were only that these bureaucrats
Would just stop and read their mail
Then I could just halt a half a minute and be able to
exhale
They're not answering must try harder
Must not let the company down
Must work hard to fill this hollow
From the business district now
Here we go now, must be spam, no that looks
Like official letterhead
But it couldn't be that really
It's got to be in my own head
What you doing, an assessment?
Well, it couldn't be of me
I'm succeeding I'm triumphant I am full of tenacity
That's the problem Not a problem

Oh, you cannot be correct

I've been working at this desk

I have placed all of the bets

Gambler

I don't know what you want from me, you're
confusing me to bits
I think that your hypocrisy is giving me the shits

You say that you don't like it when I spend money on
a dress
But you take all of your income and place it on a bet

If you want me to be serious then we'll have to have a
talk
Coz I'm telling you my darling, I'm about to fuckin
walk

I will not be a widow when my husband's still alive
And I won't be made dependant on the government to
survive

Not if I can help it, there's got to be a way
But first we need to set aside our meagre weekly pay

We can't afford to gamble, we can't afford to bet

We're not going to win the lotto, I'm not going to give
you head

Understand something my darling, you are a family
man

And the rest of us are trying to stick to the basic plan

Of getting an education, of working for some cash

And bringing up our children to know how to build a
stash

Light

Stars prickle in the night sky

The spikes of fiery light

Claiming a growing shadow

Of the outback sky at night

Like a veil across the heavens

A fabric lightly wisps

Like a brush with loving gestures

And a solemn special kiss

Maybe it's a faery

A figure up above

Who comes with great intentions

To show me all the love

The universe it beckons

It tells me it's OK

I'm not going to get in trouble

There's no need to run away

Enfin

A stillness, a fulfilled-ness
To be steady in my head
To feel the peace the inner breeze
All the wisdom that I read
I can't betray the ones before
Cannot state what others meant
But I know that in my mission
There will be no one heaven sent
Thank the wind and all the sunshine
Regard the storms and mind the hail
I cannot live for others' reasons
That to me is beyond the pale
Towards a future I am travelling
And the truth's becomes my goal
I will seek it, I will find it
I am on a fucking roll!

Biography – M Renae Dubois

Born and raised in Brisbane, Renae grew up in a household shaped by the Christian faith, as shown in her immediate family moving from the Salvation Army to the Baptist church when she was only small. But alongside that influence was music.

Her father is a musician who brought opera and live symphony into the home. Renae attended performances from childhood, absorbing the Russian composers she loves most: Mussorgsky, Shostakovich, Tchaikovsky, as well as operas, musicals, and other performances. The family did not own a television.

Renae educated herself in logic, her favourite subject at Kelvin Grove State High School, and has pursued that philosophical rigour, alongside a self-directed reading of classical literature, throughout her adult life.

At sixteen, she sustained a traumatic brain injury in a road accident that changed the course of her life and became the originating event of her literary project. She began writing within months of leaving hospital. What followed, the years of sex work, psychiatric treatment, legal battles, addiction, love, grief, and gradual artistic self-making, became the material of four books spanning thirty years.

She is also a self-taught visual artist whose paintings appear on all four book covers, constituting a visual sequence as deliberate as the literary one. M Renae Dubois is currently developing spoken word performance work and short-form video combining poetry and painting. She deeply appreciates her readers, and relishes philosophical, political, social, but ultimately language based challenging conversation.

www.ingramcontent.com/pod-product-compliance
Lightning Source LLC
Chambersburg PA
CBHW071542030726
47598CB00001B/196